This book belongs to:

_____

SB
Productions

3-Year Bible Reading Plan
Year 1 Week 1

Week starting:

☐ Monday - Genesis 1:1-2:4a & Psalm 1

☐ Tuesday - Genesis 2:4b-25 & Matthew 1:1-17

☐ Wednesday - Genesis 3:1-13 & Matthew 1:18-25

☐ Thursday - Genesis 3:14-24 & Matthew 2:1-12

☐ Friday - Genesis 4:1-16 & Matthew 2:13-15

☐ Saturday/Sunday - Genesis 4:17-26 & Matthew 2:16-23

Prayer Requests & Praise Reports

3-Year Bible Reading Plan
Year 1 Week 2

Week starting:

◻ Monday - Genesis 5 & Psalm 2

◻ Tuesday - Genesis 6 & Matthew 3:1-12

◻ Wednesday - Genesis 7 & Matthew 3:13-17

◻ Thursday - Genesis 8:1-19 & Matthew 4:1-11

◻ Friday - Genesis 8:20-9:17 & Matthew 4:12-17

◻ Saturday/Sunday - Genesis 9:18-29 & Matthew 4:18-22

Prayer Requests & Praise Reports

3-Year Bible Reading Plan
Year 1 Week 3

Week starting:

☐ Monday - Genesis 10 & Psalm 3

☐ Tuesday - Genesis 11 & Matthew 4:23-25

☐ Wednesday - Genesis 12 & Matthew 5:1-12

☐ Thursday - Genesis 13 & Matthew 5:13-20

☐ Friday - Genesis 14:1-16 & Matthew 5:21-26

☐ Saturday/Sunday - Genesis 14:17-15:21 & Matthew 5:27-30

Prayer Requests & Praise Reports

3-Year Bible Reading Plan
Year 1 Week 4

Week starting:

Monday - Genesis 16 & Psalm 4

Tuesday - Genesis 17 & Matthew 5:31-37

Wednesday - Genesis 18:1-15 & Matthew 5:38-48

Thursday - Genesis 18:16-33 & Matthew 6:1-15

Friday - Genesis 19:1-22 & Matthew 6:16-21

Saturday/Sunday - Genesis 19:23-38 & Matthew 6:22-34

Prayer Requests & Praise Reports

3-Year Bible Reading Plan
Year 1 Week 5

Week starting:

☐ Monday - Genesis 20:1-21:8 & Psalm 5

☐ Tuesday - Genesis 21:9-34 & Matthew 7:1-6

☐ Wednesday - Genesis 22:1-19 & Matthew 7:7-12

☐ Thursday - Genesis 22:20-23:20 & Matthew 7:13-20

☐ Friday - Genesis 24

☐ Saturday/Sunday - Matthew 7:21-29

Prayer Requests & Praise Reports

3-Year Bible Reading Plan
Year 1 Week 6

Week starting:

Monday - Genesis 25:1-18 & Psalm 6

Tuesday - Genesis 25:19-34 & Matthew 8:1-4

Wednesday - Genesis 26:1-25 & Matthew 8:5-13

Thursday - Genesis 26:26-35 & Matthew 8:14-22

Friday - Genesis 27:1-29 & Matthew 8:23-34

Saturday/Sunday - Genesis 27:30-28:5 & Matthew 9:1-8

Prayer Requests & Praise Reports

3-Year Bible Reading Plan
Year 1 Week 7

Week starting:

Monday - Genesis 28:6-22 & Psalm 7

Tuesday - Genesis 29:1-14 & Matthew 9:9-13

Wednesday - Genesis 29:15-30 & Matthew 9:14-17

Thursday - Genesis 29:31-30:24 & Matthew 9:19-26

Friday - Genesis 30:25-43 & Matthew 9:27-34

Saturday/Sunday - Genesis 31:1-21 & Matthew 9:35-10:4

Prayer Requests & Praise Reports

3-Year Bible Reading Plan
Year 1 Week 8

Week starting:

Monday - Genesis 31:22-42 & Psalm 8

Tuesday - Genesis 31:43-55 & Matthew 10:5-15

Wednesday - Genesis 32:1-21 & Matthew 10:16-25

Thursday - Genesis 32:22-32 & Matthew 10:26-31

Friday - Genesis 33 & Matthew 10:32-39

Saturday/Sunday - Genesis 34 & Matthew 10:40-42

Prayer Requests & Praise Reports

3-Year Bible Reading Plan
Year 1 Week 9

Week starting:

Monday - Genesis 35:1-26 & Psalm 9

Tuesday - Genesis 35:27-36:30 & Matthew 11:1-19

Wednesday - Genesis 36:31-37:11 & Matthew 11:20-24

Thursday - Genesis 37:12-36 & Matthew 11:25-30

Friday - Genesis 38 & Matthew 12:1-8

Saturday/Sunday - Genesis 39 & Matthew 12:9-21

Prayer Requests & Praise Reports

3-Year Bible Reading Plan
Year 1 Week 10

Week starting:

☐ Monday - Genesis 40 & Psalm 10

☐ Tuesday - Genesis 41:1-36 & Matthew 12:22-32

☐ Wednesday - Genesis 41:37-57 & Matthew 12:33-37

☐ Thursday - Genesis 42 & Matthew 12:38-42

☐ Friday - Genesis 43 & Matthew 12:43-50

☐ Saturday/Sunday - Genesis 44 & Matthew 13:1-9

Prayer Requests & Praise Reports

3-Year Bible Reading Plan
Year 1 Week 11

Week starting:

☐ Monday - Genesis 45 & Psalm 11

☐ Tuesday - Genesis 46 & Matthew 13:10-17

☐ Wednesday - Genesis 47 & Matthew 13:18-23

☐ Thursday - Genesis 48 & Matthew 13:24-32

☐ Friday - Genesis 49:1-28 & Matthew 13:33-35

☐ Saturday/Sunday - Genesis 49:29-50:26 & Matthew 13:36-43

Prayer Requests & Praise Reports

3-Year Bible Reading Plan
Year 1 Week 12

Week starting:

Monday - Exodus 1 & Psalm 12

Tuesday - Exodus 2:1-10 & Matthew 13:44-52

Wednesday - Exodus 2:11-25 & Matthew 13:53-14:12

Thursday - Exodus 3 & Matthew 14:13-21

Friday - Exodus 4:1-17 & Matthew 14:22-33

Saturday/Sunday - Exodus 4:18-31 & Matthew 14:34-15:9

Prayer Requests & Praise Reports

3-Year Bible Reading Plan
Year 1 Week 13

Week starting:

▢ Monday - Exodus 5:1-21 & Psalm 13

▢ Tuesday - Exodus 5:22-6:12 & Matthew 15:10-20

▢ Wednesday - Exodus 6:13-7:7 & Matthew 15:21-31

▢ Thursday - Exodus 7:8-25 & Matthew 15:32-39

▢ Friday - Exodus 8:1-19 & Matthew 16:1-12

▢ Saturday/Sunday - Exodus 8:20-9:7 & Matthew 16:13-20

Prayer Requests & Praise Reports

3-Year Bible Reading Plan
Year 1 Week 14

Week starting:

Monday - Exodus 9:8-35 & Psalm 14

Tuesday - Exodus 10:1-20 & Matthew 16:21-28

Wednesday - Exodus 10:21-11:10 & Matthew 17:1-13

Thursday - Exodus 12:1-14 & Matthew 17:14-21

Friday - Exodus 12:15-28 & Matthew 17:22-27

Saturday/Sunday - Exodus 12:29-42 & Matthew 18:1-9

Prayer Requests & Praise Reports

3-Year Bible Reading Plan
Year 1 Week 15

Week starting:

Monday - Exodus 12:43-13:10 & Psalm 15

Tuesday - Exodus 13:11-22 & Matthew 18:10-14

Wednesday - Exodus 14 & Matthew 18:15-20

Thursday - Exodus 15:1-18 & Matthew 18:21-35

Friday - Exodus 15:19-27 & Matthew 19:1-15

Saturday/Sunday - Exodus 16 & Matthew 19:16-30

Prayer Requests & Praise Reports

3-Year Bible Reading Plan
Year 1 Week 16

Week starting:

☐ Monday - Exodus 17:1-7 & Psalm 16

☐ Tuesday - Exodus 17:8-16 & Matthew 20:1-16

☐ Wednesday - Exodus 18:1-12 & Matthew 20:17-28

☐ Thursday - Exodus 18:13-27 & Matthew 20:29-34

☐ Friday - Exodus 19 & Matthew 21:1-11

☐ Saturday/Sunday - Exodus 20:1-21 & Matthew 21:12-17

Prayer Requests & Praise Reports

3-Year Bible Reading Plan
Year 1 Week 17

Week starting:

Monday - Exodus 20:22-21:11 & Psalm 17

Tuesday - Exodus 21:12-27 & Matthew 21:18-27

Wednesday - Exodus 21:28-36 & Matthew 21:28-32

Thursday - Exodus 22:1-15 & Matthew 21:33-46

Friday - Exodus 22:16-31 & Matthew 22:1-14

Saturday/Sunday - Exodus 23:1-19 & Matthew 22:15-33

Prayer Requests & Praise Reports

3-Year Bible Reading Plan
Year 1 Week 18

Week starting:

▢ Monday - Psalm 18

▢ Tuesday - Exodus 23:20-33 & Matthew 22:34-46

▢ Wednesday - Exodus 24 & Matthew 23:1-12

▢ Thursday - Exodus 25:1-22 & Matthew 23:13-28

▢ Friday - Exodus 25:23-40 & Matthew 23:29-24:2

▢ Saturday/Sunday - Exodus 26 & Matthew 24:3-14

Prayer Requests & Praise Reports

3-Year Bible Reading Plan
Year 1 Week 19

Week starting:

Monday - Exodus 27:1-28:14

Tuesday - Exodus 28:15-30 & Matthew 24:15-31

Wednesday - Exodus 28:31-43 & Matthew 24:32-44

Thursday - Exodus 29:1-37 & Matthew 24:45-51

Friday - Exodus 29:38-46 & Matthew 25:1-13

Saturday/Sunday - Exodus 30:1-10 & Matthew 25:14-30

Prayer Requests & Praise Reports

3-Year Bible Reading Plan
Year 1 Week 20

Week starting:

Monday - Exodus 30:11-21 & Psalm 19

Tuesday - Exodus 30:22-33 & Matthew 25:31-46

Wednesday - Exodus 30:34-31:11 & Matthew 26:1-13

Thursday - Exodus 31:12-18 & Matthew 26:14-25

Friday - Exodus 32 & Matthew 26:26-35

Saturday/Sunday - Exodus 33:1-11 & Matthew 26:36-46

Prayer Requests & Praise Reports

3-Year Bible Reading Plan
Year 1 Week 21

Week starting:

☐ Monday - Exodus 33:12-23 & Psalm 20

☐ Tuesday - Exodus 34:1-9 & Matthew 26:47-56

☐ Wednesday - Exodus 34:10-28 & Matthew 26:57-68

☐ Thursday - Exodus 34:29-35:3 & Matthew 26:69-27:2

☐ Friday - Exodus 35:4-19 & Matthew 27:3-14

☐ Saturday/Sunday - Exodus 35:20-29 & Matthew 27:15-26

Prayer Requests & Praise Reports

3-Year Bible Reading Plan
Year 1 Week 22

Week starting:

☐ Monday - Exodus 35:30-36:7 & Psalm 21

☐ Tuesday - Exodus 36:8-38 & Matthew 27:27-31

☐ Wednesday - Exodus 37:1-9 & Matthew 27:32-44

☐ Thursday - Exodus 37:10-16 & Matthew 27:45-61

☐ Friday - Exodus 37:17-28 & Matthew 27:62-28:10

☐ Saturday/Sunday - Exodus 37:29-38:8 & Matthew 28:11-20

Prayer Requests & Praise Reports

3-Year Bible Reading Plan
Year 1 Week 23

Week starting:

☐ Monday - Exodus 38:9-20 & Psalm 22

___

☐ Tuesday - Exodus 38:21-31 & Romans 1:1-17

___

☐ Wednesday - Exodus 39:1-21 & Romans 1:18-32

___

☐ Thursday - Exodus 39:22-43 & Romans 2:1-16

___

☐ Friday - Exodus 40:1-33 & Romans 2:17-3:8

___

☐ Saturday/Sunday - Exodus 40:34-38 & Romans 3:9-31

___

Prayer Requests & Praise Reports

3-Year Bible Reading Plan
Year 1 Week 24

Week starting:

☐ Monday - Leviticus 1 & Psalm 23

☐ Tuesday - Leviticus 2:1-3:17 & Romans 4:1-12

☐ Wednesday - Leviticus 4 & Romans 4:13-5:11

☐ Thursday - Leviticus 5:1-6:7 & Romans 5:12-21

☐ Friday - Leviticus 6:8-7:10 & Romans 6

☐ Saturday/Sunday - Leviticus 7:11-38 & Romans 7

Prayer Requests & Praise Reports

3-Year Bible Reading Plan
Year 1 Week 25

Week starting:

- [ ] Monday - Leviticus 8 & Psalm 24

- [ ] Tuesday - Leviticus 9 & Romans 8:1-17

- [ ] Wednesday - Leviticus 10 & Romans 8:18-39

- [ ] Thursday - Leviticus 11 & Romans 9:1-18

- [ ] Friday - Leviticus 12 & Romans 9:19-10:4

- [ ] Saturday/Sunday - Leviticus 13:1-46 & Romans 10:5-21

Prayer Requests & Praise Reports

3-Year Bible Reading Plan
Year 1 Week 26

Week starting:

☐ Monday - Leviticus 13:47-14:32 & Psalm 25

☐ Tuesday - Leviticus 14:33-15:33 & Romans 11:1-12

☐ Wednesday - Leviticus 16 & Romans 11:13-24

☐ Thursday - Leviticus 17 & Romans 11:25-36

☐ Friday - Leviticus 18 & Romans 12

☐ Saturday/Sunday - Leviticus 19 & Romans 13

Prayer Requests & Praise Reports

3-Year Bible Reading Plan
Year 1 Week 27

Week starting:

Monday - Leviticus 20 & Psalm 26

Tuesday - Leviticus 21 & Romans 14:1-12

Wednesday - Leviticus 22 & Romans 14:13-23

Thursday - Leviticus 23:1-14 & Romans 15:1-21

Friday - Leviticus 23:15-32 & Romans 15:22-16:16

Saturday/Sunday - Leviticus 23:33-24:4 & Romans 16:17-27

Prayer Requests & Praise Reports

3-Year Bible Reading Plan
Year 1 Week 28

Week starting:

Monday - Leviticus 24:5-23 & Psalm 27

Tuesday - Leviticus 25:1-22 & 1 Corinthians 1

Wednesday - Leviticus 25:23-38 & 1 Corinthians 2

Thursday - Leviticus 25:39-26:13 & 1 Corinthians 3

Friday - Leviticus 26:14-46 & 1 Corinthians 4

Saturday/Sunday - Leviticus 27 & 1 Corinthians 5

Prayer Requests & Praise Reports

3-Year Bible Reading Plan
Year 1 Week 29

Week starting:

☐ **Monday - Numbers 1 & Psalm 28**

☐ **Tuesday - Nimbers 2 & 1 Corinthians 6**

☐ **Wednesday - Numbers 3:1-13 & 1 Corinthians 7:1-24**

☐ **Thursday - Numbers 3:14-51 & 1 Corinthians 7:25-40**

☐ **Friday - Numbers 4:1-20 & 1 Corinthians 8**

☐ **Saturday/Sunday - Numbers 4:21-5:4 & 1 Corinthians 9**

Prayer Requests & Praise Reports

3-Year Bible Reading Plan
Year 1 Week 30

Week starting:

☐ Monday - Numbers 5:5-31 & Psalm 29

☐ Tuesday - Numbers 6:1-21 & 1 Corinthians 10:1-11:1

☐ Wednesday - Numbers 6:22-7:89 & 1 Corinthians 11:2-16

☐ Thursday - Numbers 8 & 1 Corinthians 11:17-34

☐ Friday - Numbers 9:1-14 & 1 Corinthians 12

☐ Saturday/Sunday - Numbers 9:15-23 & 1 Corinthians 13

Prayer Requests & Praise Reports

3-Year Bible Reading Plan
Year 1 Week 31

Week starting:

☐ Monday - Numbers 10:1-10 & Psalm 30

☐ Tuesday - Numbers 10:11-32 & 1 Corinthians 14:1-25

☐ Wednesday - Numbers 10:33-11:3 & 1 Corinthians 14:26-15:11

☐ Thursday - Numbers 11:4-30 & 1 Corinthians 15:12-34

☐ Friday - Numbers 11:31-12:16 & 1 Corinthians 15:35-58

☐ Saturday/Sunday - Numbers 13 & 1 Corinthians 16

Prayer Requests & Praise Reports

3-Year Bible Reading Plan
Year 1 Week 32

Week starting:

Monday - Numbers 14:1-25 & Psalm 31

Tuesday - Numbers 14:26-45 & 2 Corinthians 1:1-11

Wednesday - Numbers 15:1-31 & 2 Corinthians 1:12-2:4

Thursday - Numbers 15:32-41 & 2 Corinthians 2:5-17

Friday - Numbers 16:1-35 & 2 Corinthians 3

Saturday/Sunday - Numbers 16:36-50 & 2 Corinthians 4:1-5:10

Prayer Requests & Praise Reports

3-Year Bible Reading Plan
Year 1 Week 33

Week starting:

☐ Monday - Numbers 17 & Psalm 32

☐ Tuesday - Numbers 18:1-7 & 2 Corinthians 5:11-6:13

☐ Wednesday - Numbers 18:8-20 & 2 Corinthians 6:14-7:1

☐ Thursday - Numbers 18:21-32 & 2 Corinthians 7:2-16

☐ Friday - Numbers 19:1-10 & 2 Corinthians 8

☐ Saturday/Sunday - Numbers 19:11-22 & 2 Corinthians 9

Prayer Requests & Praise Reports

3-Year Bible Reading Plan
Year 1 Week 34

Week starting:

☐ Monday - Numbers 20:1-21 & Psalm 33

☐ Tuesday - Numbers 20:22-21:20 & 2 Corinthians 10

☐ Wednesday - Numbers 21:21-35 & 2 Corinthians 11:1-15

☐ Thursday - Numbers 22:1-21 & 2 Corinthians 11:16-33

☐ Friday - Numbers 22:22-40 & 2 Corinthians 12:1-10

☐ Saturday/Sunday - Numbers 22:41-23:12 & 2 Corin. 12:11-13:13

Prayer Requests & Praise Reports

3-Year Bible Reading Plan
Year 1 Week 35

Week starting:

Monday - Numbers 23:13-26 & Psalm 34

Tuesday - Numbers 23:27-24:13 & Mark 1:1-8

Wednesday - Numbers 24:14-25:18 & Mark 1:9-20

Thursday - Numbers 26 & Mark 1:21-28

Friday - Numbers 27:1-11 & Mark 1:29-39

Saturday/Sunday - Numbers 27:12-28:10 & Mark 1:40-45

Prayer Requests & Praise Reports

3-Year Bible Reading Plan
Year 1 Week 36

Week starting:

Monday - Numbers 28:11-25 & Psalm 35

Tuesday - Numbers 28:26-29:11 & Mark 2:1-12

Wednesday - Numbers 29:12-40 & Mark 2:13-17

Thursday - Numbers 30 & Mark 2:18-28

Friday - Numbers 31:1-24 & Mark 3:1-6

Saturday/Sunday - Numbers 31:25-54 & Mark 3:7-19

Prayer Requests & Praise Reports

3-Year Bible Reading Plan
Year 1 Week 37

Week starting:

☐ **Monday - Numbers 32 & Psalm 36**

☐ **Tuesday - Numbers 33:1-49 & Mark 3:20-30**

☐ **Wednesday - Numbers 33:50-34:15 & Mark 3:31-4:9**

☐ **Thursday - Numbers 34:16-35:8 & Mark 4:10-12**

☐ **Friday - Numbers 35:9-34 & Mark 4:13-20**

☐ **Saturday/Sunday - Numbers 36 & Mark 4:21-25**

Prayer Requests & Praise Reports

3-Year Bible Reading Plan
Year 1 Week 38

Week starting:

☐ Monday - Deuteronomy 1:1-8 & Psalm 37

☐ Tuesday - Deuteronomy 1:9-18 & Mark 4:26-34

☐ Wednesday - Deuteronomy 1:19-45 & Mark 4:35-41

☐ Thursday - Deuteronomy 1:46-2:25 & Mark 5:1-20

☐ Friday - Deuteronomy 2:26-3:11 & Mark 5:21-43

☐ Saturday/Sunday - Deuteronomy 3:12-29 & Mark 6:1-6

Prayer Requests & Praise Reports

3-Year Bible Reading Plan
Year 1 Week 39

Week starting:

☐ Monday - Deuteronomy 4:1-14 & Psalm 38

☐ Tuesday - Deuteronomy 4:15-40 & Mark 6:7-13

☐ Wednesday - Deuteronomy 4:41-5:22 & Mark 6:14-29

☐ Thursday - Deuteronomy 5:23-6:9 & Mark 6:30-44

☐ Friday - Deuteronomy 6:10-7:11 & Mark 6:45-52

☐ Saturday/Sunday - Deuteronomy 7:12-8:10 & Mark 6:53-7:13

Prayer Requests & Praise Reports

3-Year Bible Reading Plan
Year 1 Week 40

Week starting:

☐ Monday - Deuteronomy 8:11-20 & Psalm 39

☐ Tuesday - Deuteronomy 9 & Mark 7:14-23

☐ Wednesday - Deuteronomy 10:1-11:7 & Mark 7:24-37

☐ Thursday - Deuteronomy 11:8-32 & Mark 8:1-13

☐ Friday - Deuteronomy 12:1-28 & Mark8:14-26

☐ Saturday/Sunday - Deuteronomy 12:29-13:18 & Mark 8:27-9:1

Prayer Requests & Praise Reports

3-Year Bible Reading Plan
Year 1 Week 41

Week starting:

☐ Monday - Deuteronomy 14:1-21 & Psalm 40

☐ Tuesday - Deuteronomy 14:22-29 & Mark 9:2-13

☐ Wednesday - Deuteronomy 15:1-11 & Mark 9:14-29

☐ Thursday - Deuteronomy 15:12-23 & Mark 9:30-41

☐ Friday - Deuteronomy 16:1-8 & Mark 9:42-50

☐ Saturday/Sunday - Deuteronomy 16:9-17 & Mark 10:1-16

Prayer Requests & Praise Reports

3-Year Bible Reading Plan
Year 1 Week 42

Week starting:

◻ Monday - Deuteronomy 16:18-17:13 & Psalm 41

◻ Tuesday - Deuteronomy 17:14-18:8 & Mark 10:17-31

◻ Wednesday - Deuteronomy 18:9-22 & Mark 10:32-34

◻ Thursday - Deuteronomy 19:1-13 & Mark 10:35-45

◻ Friday - Deuteronomy 19:14-21 & Mark 10:46-52

◻ Saturday/Sunday - Deuteronomy 20 & Mark 11:1-11

Prayer Requests & Praise Reports

3-Year Bible Reading Plan
Year 1 Week 43

Week starting:

☐ Monday - Deuteronomy 21:1-21 & Psalm 42

☐ Tuesday - Deuteronomy 21:22-22:12 & Mark 11:12-19

☐ Wednesday - Deuteronomy 22:13-30 & Mark 11:20-33

☐ Thursday - Deuteronomy 23 & Mark 12:1-12

☐ Friday - Deuteronomy 24:1-25:4 & Mark 12:13-17

☐ Saturday/Sunday - Deuteronomy 25:5-26:15 & Mark 12:18-27

Prayer Requests & Praise Reports

3-Year Bible Reading Plan
Year 1 Week 44

Week starting:

Monday - Deuteronomy 26:16-27:26 & Psalm 43

Tuesday - Deuteronomy 28:1-14 & Mark 12:28-37

Wednesday - Deuteronomy 28:15-68

Thursday - Mark 12:38-13:13

Friday - Deuteronomy 29 & Mark 13:14-27

Saturday/Sunday - Deuteronomy 30:1-31:8 & Mark 13:28-37

Prayer Requests & Praise Reports

3-Year Bible Reading Plan
Year 1 Week 45

Week starting:

Monday - Deuteronomy 31:9-29 & Psalm 44

Tuesday - Deuteronomy 31:30-32:44

Wednesday - Mark 14:1-21

Thursday - Deuteronomy 32:45-52 & Mark 14:22-26

Friday - Deuteronomy 33 & Mark 14:27-31

Saturday/Sunday - Deuteronomy 34 & Mark 14:32-42

Prayer Requests & Praise Reports

3-Year Bible Reading Plan
Year 1 Week 46

Week starting:

☐ Monday - Joshua 1 & Psalm 45

☐ Tuesday - Joshua 2 & Mark 14:43-52

☐ Wednesday - Joshua 3 & Mark 14:53-65

☐ Thursday - Joshua 4:1-5:1 & Mark 14:66-72

☐ Friday - Joshua 5:2-15 & Mark 15:1-5

☐ Saturday/Sunday - Joshua 6 & Mark 15:6-20

Prayer Requests & Praise Reports

3-Year Bible Reading Plan
Year 1 Week 47

Week starting:

Monday - Joshua 7 & Psalm 46

Tuesday - Joshua 8:1-29 & Mark 15:21-32

Wednesday - Joshua 8:30-35 & Mark 15:33-41

Thursday - Joshua 9 & Mark 15:42-47

Friday - Joshua 10:1-15 & Mark 16:1-13

Saturday/Sunday - Joshua 10:16-27 & Mark 16:14-20

Prayer Requests & Praise Reports

3-Year Bible Reading Plan
Year 1 Week 48

Week starting:

☐ Monday - Joshua 10:28-43 & Psalm 47

☐ Tuesday - Joshua 11:1-15 & Galatians 1:1-10

☐ Wednesday - Joshua 11:16-12:6 & Galatians 1:11-24

☐ Thursday - Joshua 12:7-13:7 & Galatians 2

☐ Friday - Joshua 13:8-23 & Galatians 3:1-14

☐ Saturday/Sunday - Joshua 13:24-14:5 & Galatians 3:15-4:7

Prayer Requests & Praise Reports

3-Year Bible Reading Plan
Year 1 Week 49

Week starting:

☐ Monday - Joshua 14:6-15 & Psalm 48

☐ Tuesday - Joshua 15:1-19 & Galatians 4:8-20

☐ Wednesday - Joshua 15:20-63 & Galatians 4:21-31

☐ Thursday - Joshua 16 & Galatians 5:1-15

☐ Friday - Joshua 17:1-13 & Galatians 5:16-26

☐ Saturday/Sunday - Joshua 17:14-18:10 & Galatians 6

Prayer Requests & Praise Reports

3-Year Bible Reading Plan
Year 1 Week 50

Week starting:

Monday - Joshua 18:11-28 & Psalm 49

Tuesday - Joshua 19:1-16 & Ephesians 1:1-14

Wednesday - Joshua 19:17-39 & Ephesians 1:15-23

Thursday - Joshua 19:40-51 & Ephesians 2:1-10

Friday - Joshua 20 & Ephesians 2:11-22

Saturday/Sunday - Joshua 21:1-42 & Ephesians 3

Prayer Requests & Praise Reports

3-Year Bible Reading Plan
Year 1 Week 51

Week starting:

☐ Monday - Joshua 21:43-22:9 & Psalm 50

☐ Tuesday - Joshua 22:10-34

☐ Wednesday - Ephesians 4

☐ Thursday - Joshua 23 & Ephesians 5:1-20

☐ Friday - Joshua 24:1-28 & Ephesians 5:21-6:9

☐ Saturday/Sunday - Joshua 24:29-33 & Ephesians 6:10-24

Prayer Requests & Praise Reports

3-Year Bible Reading Plan
Year 1 Week 52

Week starting:

Monday - *As the Lord leads*

Tuesday - *As the Lord leads*

Wednesday - *As the Lord leads*

Thursday - *As the Lord leads*

Friday - *As the Lord leads*

Saturday/Sunday - *As the Lord leads*

Prayer Requests & Praise Reports

3-Year Bible Reading Plan
Year 2 Week 1

Week starting:

☐ Monday - Judges 1:1-10 & Psalm 51

☐ Tuesday - Judges 1:11-21 & Luke 1:1-25

☐ Wednesday - Judges 1:22-36 & Luke 1:26-38

☐ Thursday - Judges 2:1-10 & Luke 1:39-56

☐ Friday - Judges 2:11-23 & Luke 1:57-66

☐ Saturday/Sunday - Judges 3:1-11 & Luke 1:67-2:7

Prayer Requests & Praise Reports

3-Year Bible Reading Plan
Year 2 Week 2

Week starting:

Monday - Judges 3:12-31 & Psalm 52

Tuesday - Judges 4 & Luke 2:8-21

Wednesday - Judges 5 & Luke 2:22-38

Thursday - Judges 6 & Luke 2:39-52

Friday - Judges 7 & Luke 3:1-20

Saturday/Sunday - Judges 8:1-28 & Luke 3:21-38

Prayer Requests & Praise Reports

3-Year Bible Reading Plan
Year 2 Week 3

Week starting:

Monday - Judges 8:29-35 & Psalm 53

Tuesday - Judges 9 & Luke 4:1-15

Wednesday - Judges 10:1-11:33 & Luke 4:16-30

Thursday - Judges 11:34-12:15 & Luke 4:31-41

Friday - Judges 13 & Luke 4:42-5:11

Saturday/Sunday - Judges 14:1-15:8 & Luke 5:12-16

Prayer Requests & Praise Reports

3-Year Bible Reading Plan
Year 2 Week 4

Week starting:

Monday - Judges 15:9-20 & Psalm 54

Tuesday - Judges 16:1-22 & Luke 5:17-32

Wednesday - Judges 16:23-17:13 & Luke 5:33-6:5

Thursday - Judges 18 & Luke 6:6-16

Friday - Judges 19 & Luke 6:17-26

Saturday/Sunday - Judges 20:1-17 & Luke 6:27-42

Prayer Requests & Praise Reports

3-Year Bible Reading Plan
Year 2 Week 5

Week starting:

☐ Monday - Judges 20:18-48 & Psalm 55

☐ Tuesday - Judges 21 & Luke 6:43-49

☐ Wednesday - Ruth 1 & Luke 7:1-17

☐ Thursday - Ruth 2 & Luke 7:18-35

☐ Friday - Ruth 3 & Luke 7:36-50

☐ Saturday/Sunday - Ruth 4 & Luke 8:1-8

Prayer Requests & Praise Reports

3-Year Bible Reading Plan
Year 2 Week 6

Week starting:

Monday - Isaiah 1:1-20 & Psalm 56

Tuesday - Isaiah 1:21-31 & Luke 8:9-15

Wednesday - Isaiah 2:1-5 & Luke 8:16-21

Thursday - Isaiah 2:6-22 & Luke 8:22-25

Friday - Isaiah 3:1-12 & Luke 8:26-39

Saturday/Sunday - Isaiah 3:13-4:1 & Luke 8:40-56

Prayer Requests & Praise Reports

3-Year Bible Reading Plan
Year 2 Week 7

Week starting:

☐ Monday - Isaiah 4:2-6 & Psalm 57

☐ Tuesday - Isaiah 5:1-7 & Luke 9:1-9

☐ Wednesday - Isaiah 5:8-30 & Luke 9:10-17

☐ Thursday - Isaiah 6 & Luke 9:18-27

☐ Friday - Isaiah 7:1-9 & Luke 9:28-36

☐ Saturday/Sunday - Isaiah 7:10-25 & Luke 9:37-45

Prayer Requests & Praise Reports

3-Year Bible Reading Plan
Year 2 Week 8

Week starting:

☐ Monday - Isaiah 8:1-10 & Psalm 58

☐ Tuesday - Isaiah 8:11-22 & Luke 9:46-56

☐ Wednesday - Isaiah 9:1-6 & Luke 9:57-10:12

☐ Thursday - Isaiah 9:7-10:4 & Luke 10:13-16

☐ Friday - Isaiah 10:5-19 & Luke 10:17-24

☐ Saturday/Sunday - Isaiah 10:20-27 & Luke 10:25-37

Prayer Requests & Praise Reports

3-Year Bible Reading Plan
Year 2 Week 9

Week starting:

☐ Monday - Isaiah 10:28-11:9 & Psalm 59

☐ Tuesday - Isaiah 11:10-16 & Luke 10:38-42

☐ Wednesday - Isaiah 12 & Luke 11:1-13

☐ Thursday - Isaiah 13 & Luke 11:14-23

☐ Friday - Isaiah 14:1-21 & Luke 11:24-32

☐ Saturday/Sunday - Isaiah 14:22-27 & Luke 11:33-36

Prayer Requests & Praise Reports

3-Year Bible Reading Plan
Year 2 Week 10

Week starting:

Monday - Isaiah 14:28-32 & Psalm 60

Tuesday - Isaiah 15 & Luke 11:37-54

Wednesday - Isaiah 16 & Luke 12:1-12

Thursday - Isaiah 17 & Luke 12:13-21

Friday - Isaiah 18:1-19:15 & Luke 12:22-31

Saturday/Sunday - Isaiah 19:16-25 & Luke 12:32-40

Prayer Requests & Praise Reports

3-Year Bible Reading Plan
Year 2 Week 11

Week starting:

☐ Monday - Isaiah 20 & Psalm 61

☐ Tuesday - Isaiah 21 & Luke 12:41-53

☐ Wednesday - Isaiah 22:1-14 & Luke 12:54-13:5

☐ Thursday - Isaiah 22:15-25 & Luke 13:6-17

☐ Friday - Isaiah 23 & Luke 13:18-30

☐ Saturday/Sunday - Isaiah 24 & Luke 13:31-35

Prayer Requests & Praise Reports

3-Year Bible Reading Plan
Year 2 Week 12

Week starting:

Monday - Isaiah 25:1-5 & Psalm 62

Tuesday - Isaiah 25:6-12 & Luke 14:1-6

Wednesday - Isaiah 26:1-19 & Luke 14:7-14

Thursday - Isaiah 26:20-27:11 & Luke 14:15-24

Friday - Isaiah 27:12-28:6 & Luke 14:25-33

Saturday/Sunday - Isaiah 28:7-22 & Luke 14:34-15:10

Prayer Requests & Praise Reports

3-Year Bible Reading Plan
Year 2 Week 13

Week starting:

Monday - Isaiah 28:23-29 & Psalm 63

Tuesday - Isaiah 29:1-14 & Luke 15:11-32

Wednesday - Isaiah 29:15-24 & Luke 16:1-13

Thursday - Isaiah 30:1-7 & Luke 16:14-18

Friday - Isaiah 30:8-18 & Luke 16:19-17:4

Saturday/Sunday - Isaiah 30:19-33 & Luke 17:5-19

Prayer Requests & Praise Reports

3-Year Bible Reading Plan
Year 2 Week 14

Week starting:

☐ Monday - Isaiah 31 & Psalm 64

☐ Tuesday - Isaiah 32 & Luke 17:20-37

☐ Wednesday - Isaiah 33:1-16 & Luke 18:1-8

☐ Thursday - Isaiah 33:17-24 & Luke 18:9-17

☐ Friday - Isaiah 34 & Luke 18:18-34

☐ Saturday/Sunday - Isaiah 35 & Luke 18:35-43

Prayer Requests & Praise Reports

3-Year Bible Reading Plan
Year 2 Week 15

Week starting:

☐ Monday - Isaiah 36 & Psalm 65

☐ Tuesday - Isaiah 37:1-7 & Luke 19:1-10

☐ Wednesday - Isaiah 37:8-20 & Luke 19:11-27

☐ Thursday - Isaiah 37:21-38 & Luke 19:28-40

☐ Friday - Isaiah 38 & Luke 19:41-48

☐ Saturday/Sunday - Isaiah 39:1-40:11 & Luke 20:1-8

Prayer Requests & Praise Reports

3-Year Bible Reading Plan
Year 2 Week 16

Week starting:

Monday - Isaiah 40:12-31 & Psalm 66

Tuesday - Isaiah 41:1-20 & Luke 20:9-18

Wednesday - Isaiah 41:21-29 & Luke 20:19-26

Thursday - Isaiah 42:1-9 & Luke 20:27-44

Friday - Isaiah 42:10-25 & Luke 20:45-21:6

Saturday/Sunday - Isaiah 43:1-13 & Luke 21:7-24

Prayer Requests & Praise Reports

3-Year Bible Reading Plan
Year 2 Week 17

Week starting:

☐ Monday - Isaiah 43:14-28 & Psalm 67

☐ Tuesday - Isaiah 44:1-20 & Luke 21:25-38

☐ Wednesday - Isaiah 44:21-28 & Luke 22:1-13

☐ Thursday - Isaiah 45:1-8 & Luke 22:14-30

☐ Friday - Isaiah 45:9-19 & Luke 22:31-38

☐ Saturday/Sunday - Isaiah 45:20-46:13 & Luke 22:39-53

Prayer Requests & Praise Reports

3-Year Bible Reading Plan
Year 2 Week 18

Week starting:

Monday - Isaiah 47 & Psalm 68

Tuesday - Isaiah 48:1-11 & Luke 22:54-62

Wednesday - Isaiah 48:12-22 & Luke 22:63-71

Thursday - Isaiah 49:1-7 & Luke 23:1-12

Friday - Isaiah 49:8-50:3 & Luke 23:13-25

Saturday/Sunday - Isaiah 50:4-11 & Luke 23:26-43

Prayer Requests & Praise Reports

3-Year Bible Reading Plan
Year 2 Week 19

Week starting:

- [ ] Monday - Isaiah 51:1-16 & Psalm 69

- [ ] Tuesday - Isaiah 51:17-23 & Luke 23:44-49

- [ ] Wednesday - Isaiah 52:1-12 & Luke 23:50-56

- [ ] Thursday - Isaiah 52:13-53:12 & Luke 24:1-12

- [ ] Friday - Isaiah 54 & Luke 24:13-35

- [ ] Saturday/Sunday - Isaiah 55 & Luke 24:36-53

Prayer Requests & Praise Reports

3-Year Bible Reading Plan
Year 2 Week 20

Week starting:

☐ Monday - Isaiah 56 & Psalm 70

☐ Tuesday - Isaiah 57 & Job 1:1-2:13

☐ Wednesday - Isaiah 58 & Job 3:1-5:27

☐ Thursday - Isaiah 59:1-8 & Job 6:1-7:21

☐ Friday - Isaiah 59:9-21 & Job 8

☐ Saturday/Sunday - Isaiah 60 & Job 9:1-10:22

Prayer Requests & Praise Reports

3-Year Bible Reading Plan
Year 2 Week 21

Week starting:

☐ Monday - Isaiah 61:1-62:12 & Psalm 71

☐ Tuesday - Isaiah 63:1-14 & Job 11

☐ Wednesday - Isaiah 63:15-64:12 7 Job 12:1-14:22

☐ Thursday - Isaiah 65:1-16 & Job 15

☐ Friday - Isaiah 65:17-25 & Job 16:1-18:21

☐ Saturday/Sunday - Isaiah 66 & Job 19:1-20:29

Prayer Requests & Praise Reports

3-Year Bible Reading Plan
Year 2 Week 22

Week starting:

☐ Monday - 1 Samuel 1:1-18 & Psalm 72

☐ Tuesday - 1 Samuel 1:19-2:11 & Job 21:1-22:30

☐ Wednesday - 1 Samuel 2:12-26 & Job 23:1-24:17

☐ Thursday - 1 Samuel 2:27-3:21 & Job 24:18-27:12

☐ Friday - 1 Samuel 4:1-11 & Job 27:13-28:28

☐ Saturday/Sunday - 1 Samuel 4:12-5:12 & Job 29:1-31:40

Prayer Requests & Praise Reports

3-Year Bible Reading Plan
Year 2 Week 23

Week starting:

☐ **Monday - 1 Samuel 6:1-19 & Psalm 73**

☐ **Tuesday - Job 32:1-37:24**

☐ **Wednesday - 1 Samuel 6:20-7:17**

☐ **Thursday - 1 Samuel 8 & Job 38:1-40:2**

☐ **Friday - 1 Samuel 9:1-25 & Job 40:3-42:6**

☐ **Saturday/Sunday - 1 Samuel 9:26-10:16 & Job 42:7-17**

Prayer Requests & Praise Reports

3-Year Bible Reading Plan
Year 2 Week 24

Week starting:

Monday - 1 Samuel 10:17-11:15 & Psalm 74

Tuesday - 1 Samuel 12 & Acts 1

Wednesday - 1 Samuel 13 & Acts 2:1-13

Thursday - 1 Samuel 14:1-15 & Acts 2:14-47

Friday - 1 Samuel 14:16-23 & Acts 3:1-4:22

Saturday/Sunday - 1 Samuel 14:24-46 & Acts 4:23-31

Prayer Requests & Praise Reports

3-Year Bible Reading Plan
Year 2 Week 25

Week starting:

☐ Monday - 1 Samuel 14:47-15:9 & Psalm 75

☐ Tuesday - 1 Samuel 15:10-16:13 & Acts 4:32-5:16

☐ Wednesday - 1 Samuel 16:14-17:11 & Acts 5:17-6:7

☐ Thursday - 1 Samuel 17:12-40 & Acts 6:8-15

☐ Friday - Acts 7:1-8:1a

☐ Saturday/Sunday - 1 Samuel 17:41-18:30

Prayer Requests & Praise Reports

3-Year Bible Reading Plan
Year 2 Week 26

Week starting:

☐ Monday - 1 Samuel 19 & Psalm 76

☐ Tuesday - 1 Samuel 20 & Acts 8:1b-25

☐ Wednesday - 1 Samuel 21 & Acts 8:26-40

☐ Thursday - 1 Samuel 22 & Acts 9:1-19a

☐ Friday - 1 Samuel 23 & Acts 9:19b-25

☐ Saturday/Sunday - 1 Samuel 24:1-25:1a & Acts 9:26-43

Prayer Requests & Praise Reports

3-Year Bible Reading Plan
Year 2 Week 27

Week starting:

☐ Monday - 1 Samuel 25:1b-44 & Psalm 77

☐ Tuesday - 1 Samuel 26 & Acts 10:1-33

☐ Wednesday - 1 Samuel 27:1-28:2 & Acts 10:34-48

☐ Thursday - 1 Samuel 28:3-25 & Acts 11:1-18

☐ Friday - 1 Samuel 29 & Acts 11:19-12:5

☐ Saturday/Sunday - 1 Samuel 30:1-31:13 & Acts 12:6-19

Prayer Requests & Praise Reports

3-Year Bible Reading Plan
Year 2 Week 28

Week starting:

Monday - Psalm 78

Tuesday - 2 Samuel 1:1-16 & Acts 12:20-13:12

Wednesday - 2 Samuel 1:17-2:11 & Acts 13:13-52

Thursday - 2 Samuel 2:12-3:1 & Acts 14:1-7

Friday - 2 Samuel 3:2-21 & Acts 14:8-28

Saturday/Sunday - 2 Samuel 3:22-39 & Acts 15:1-21

Prayer Requests & Praise Reports

3-Year Bible Reading Plan
Year 2 Week 29

Week starting:

- Monday - 2 Samuel 4:1-5:25

- Tuesday - 2 Samuel 6 & Acts 15:22-35

- Wednesday - 2 Samuel 7:1-17 & Acts 15:36-16:10

- Thursday - 2 Samuel 7:18-29 & Acts 16:11-40

- Friday - 2 Samuel 8 & Acts 17:1-9

- Saturday/Sunday - 2 Samuel 9 & Acts 17:10-15

Prayer Requests & Praise Reports

3-Year Bible Reading Plan
Year 2 Week 30

Week starting:

☐ Monday - 2 Samuel 10 & Psalm 79

☐ Tuesday - 2 Samuel 11 & Acts 17:16-34

☐ Wednesday - 2 Samuel 12:1-15 & Acts 18

☐ Thursday - 2 Samuel 12:16-31 & Acts 19:1-20

☐ Friday - 2 Samuel 13:1-22 & Acts 19:21-41

☐ Saturday/Sunday - 2 Samuel 13:23-39 & Acts 20:1-16

Prayer Requests & Praise Reports

3-Year Bible Reading Plan
Year 2 Week 31

Week starting:

☐ Monday - 2 Samuel 14:1-24 & Psalm 80

☐ Tuesday - 2 Samuel 14:25-15:12 & Acts 20:17-38

☐ Wednesday - 2 Samuel 15:13-37 & Acts 21:1-16

☐ Thursday - 2 Samuel 16:1-14 & Acts 21:17-36

☐ Friday - 2 Samuel 16:15-17:14 & Acts 21:37-22:16

☐ Saturday/Sunday - 2 Samuel 17:15-29 & Acts 22:17-29

Prayer Requests & Praise Reports

3-Year Bible Reading Plan
Year 2 Week 32

Week starting:

Monday - 2 Samuel 18:1-18 & Psalm 81

Tuesday - 2 Samuel 18:19-33 & Acts 22:30-23:22

Wednesday - 2 Samuel 19:1-18 & Acts 23:23-24:9

Thursday - 2 Samuel 19:18-30 & Acts 24:10-27

Friday - 2 Samuel 19:31-43 & Acts 25:1-12

Saturday/Sunday - 2 Samuel 20:1-22 & Acts 25:13-26:11

Prayer Requests & Praise Reports

3-Year Bible Reading Plan
Year 2 Week 33

Week starting:

☐ Monday - 2 Samuel 20:23-21:14 & Psalm 82

☐ Tuesday - 2 Samuel 21:15-22 & Acts 26:12-18

☐ Wednesday - 2 Samuel 22 & Acts 26:19-32

☐ Thursday - 2 Samuel 23:1-7 & Acts 27:1-12

☐ Friday - 2 Samuel 23:8-39 & Acts 27:13-28:10

☐ Saturday/Sunday - 2 Samuel 24 & Acts 28:11-31

Prayer Requests & Praise Reports

3-Year Bible Reading Plan
Year 2 Week 34

Week starting:

Monday - Jeremiah 1:1-10 & Psalm 83

Tuesday - Jeremiah 1:11-2:3 & Proverbs 1

Wednesday - Jeremiah 2:4-13 & Proverbs 2

Thursday - Jeremiah 2:14-19 & Proverbs 3

Friday - Jeremiah 2:20-25 & Proverbs 4:1-5:23

Saturday/Sunday - Jeemiah 2:26-3:5 & Proverbs 6:1-19

Prayer Requests & Praise Reports

3-Year Bible Reading Plan
Year 2 Week 35

Week starting:

☐ Monday - Jeremiah 3:6-18 & Psalm 84

☐ Tuesday - Jeremiah 3:19-25 & Proverbs 6:20-7:27

☐ Wednesday - Jeremiah 4:1-12 & Proverbs 8

☐ Thursday - Jeremiah 4:13-22 & Proverbs 9

☐ Friday - Jeremiah 4:23-31 & Proverbs 10

☐ Saturday/Sunday - Jeremiah 5:1-11 & Proverbs 11

Prayer Requests & Praise Reports

3-Year Bible Reading Plan
Year 2 Week 36

Week starting:

☐ Monday - Jeremiah 5:12-19 & Psalm 85

☐ Tuesday - Jeremiah 5:20-31 & Proverbs 12

☐ Wednesday - Jeremiah 6:1-8 & Proverbs 13

☐ Thursday - Jeremiah 6:9-15 & Proverbs 14

☐ Friday - Jeremiah 6:16-30 & Proverbs 15

☐ Saturday/Sunday - Jeremiah 7:1-15 & Proverbs 16

Prayer Requests & Praise Reports

3-Year Bible Reading Plan
Year 2 Week 37

Week starting:

☐ Monday - Jeremiah 7:16-28 & Psalm 86

☐ Tuesday - Jeremiah 7:29-8:3 & Proverbs 17:1-27

☐ Wednesday - Jeremiah 8:4-17 & Proverbs 18

☐ Thursday - Jeremiah 8:18-9:16 & Proverbs 19

☐ Friday - Jeremiah 9:17-26 & Proverbs 20

☐ Saturday/Sunday - Jeremiah 10:1-11 & Proverbs 21

Prayer Requests & Praise Reports

3-Year Bible Reading Plan
Year 2 Week 38

Week starting:

■ Monday - Jeremiah 10:12-16 & Psalm 87

■ Tuesday - Jeremiah 10:17-25 & Proverbs 22

■ Wednesday - Jeremiah 11:1-17 & Proverbs 23:1-18

■ Thursday - Jeremiah 11:18-12:6 & Proverbs 23:19-24:22

■ Friday - Jeremiah 12:7-17 & Proverbs 24:23-34

■ Saturday/Sunday - Jeremiah 13:1-14 & Proverbs 25

Prayer Requests & Praise Reports

3-Year Bible Reading Plan
Year 2 Week 39

Week starting:

☐ Monday - Jeremiah 13:15-27 & Psalm 88

☐ Tuesday - Jeremiah 14:1-18 & Proverbs 26

☐ Wednesday - Jeremiah 14:19-22 & Proverbs 27

☐ Thursday - Jeremiah 15:1-9 & Proverbs 28

☐ Friday - Jeremiah 15:10-21 & Proverbs 29:1-30:6

☐ Saturday/Sunday - Jeremiah 16:1-13 & Proverbs 30:7-31:31

Prayer Requests & Praise Reports

3-Year Bible Reading Plan
Year 2 Week 40

Week starting:

Monday - Jermeiah 16:14-21 & Psalm 89

Tuesday - Jeremiah 17:1-4 & Philippians 1:1-11

Wednesday - Jeremiah 17:5-13 & Philippians 1:12-30

Thursday - Jeremiah 17:14-18 & Philippians 2:1-18

Friday - Jeremiah 17:19-27 & Philippians 2:19-3:21

Saturday/Sunday - Jeremiah 18:1-17 & Philippians 4

Prayer Requests & Praise Reports

3-Year Bible Reading Plan
Year 2 Week 41

Week starting:

☐ **Monday - Jeremiah 18:18-23 & Psalm 90**

☐ **Tuesday - Jeremiah 19 & Colossians 1:1-14**

☐ **Wednesday - Jeremiah 20 & Colossians 1:15-2:5**

☐ **Thursday - Jeremiah 21:1-10 & Colossians 2:6-3:4**

☐ **Friday - Jeremiah 21:11-22:12 & Colossians 3:5-17**

☐ **Saturday/Sunday - Jeremiah 22:13-23 & Colossians 3:18-4:18**

Prayer Requests & Praise Reports

3-Year Bible Reading Plan
Year 2 Week 42

Week starting:

☐ Monday - Jeremiah 22:24-23:8 & Psalm 91

☐ Tuesday - Jeremiah 23:9-32 & 1 Thessalonians 1:1-2:16

☐ Wednesday - Jeremiah 23:33-40 & 1 Thessalonians 2:17-4:12

☐ Thursday - Jeremiah 24 & 1 Thessalonians 4:13-5:28

☐ Friday - Jeremiah 25:1-14 & 2 Thessalonians 1:1-2:12

☐ Saturday/Sunday - Jeremiah 25:15-38 & 2 Thes. 2:13-3:18

Prayer Requests & Praise Reports

3-Year Bible Reading Plan
Year 2 Week 43

Week starting:

☐ Monday - Jeremiah 26 & Psalm 92

☐ Tuesday - Jeremiah 27 & 1 Timothy 1

☐ Wednesday - Jeremiah 28 & 1 Timothy 2:1-3:7

☐ Thursday - Jeremiah 29:1-23 & 1 Timothy 3:8-4:16

☐ Friday - Jeremiah 29:24-32 & 1 Timothy 5:1-6:2

☐ Saturday/Sunday - Jeremiah 30 & 1 Timothy 6:2-21

Prayer Requests & Praise Reports

3-Year Bible Reading Plan
Year 2 Week 44

Week starting:

Monday - Jeremiah 31:1-14 & Psalm 93

_____

_____

_____

Tuesday - Jeremiah 31:15-22 & 2 Timothy 1

_____

_____

_____

Wednesday - Jeremiah 31:23-40 & 2 Timothy 2:1-13

_____

_____

_____

Thursday - Jeremiah 32:1-15 & 2 Timothy 2:14-26

_____

_____

_____

Friday - Jeremiah 32:16-44 & 2 Timothy 3:1-9

_____

_____

_____

Saturday/Sunday - Jeremiah 33:1-34:7 & 2 Timothy 3:10-4:22

_____

_____

_____

Prayer Requests & Praise Reports

_____

_____

_____

3-Year Bible Reading Plan
Year 2 Week 45

Week starting:

☐ Monday - Jeremiah 34:8-22 & Psalm 94

☐ Tuesday - Jeremiah 35 & Titus 1

☐ Wednesday - Jeremiah 36:1-10 & Titus 2

☐ Thursday - Jeremiah 36:11-32 & Titus 3

☐ Friday - Jeremiah 37 & Philemon 1-7

☐ Saturday/Sunday - Jeremiah 38:1-13 & Philemon 8-25

Prayer Requests & Praise Reports

3-Year Bible Reading Plan
Year 2 Week 46

Week starting:

Monday - Jeremiah 38:14-28 & Psalm 95

Tuesday - Jeremiah 39:1-14 & Ecclesiastes 1:1-11

Wednesday - Jeremiah 39:15-40:12 & Ecclesiastes 1:12-2:26

Thursday - Jeremiah 40:13-41:18 & Ecclesiastes 3:1-15

Friday - Jeremiah 42:1-6 & Ecclesiastes 3:16-5:6

Saturday/Sunday - Jeremiah 42:7-22 & Ecclesiastes 5:7-6:12

Prayer Requests & Praise Reports

3-Year Bible Reading Plan
Year 2 Week 47

Week starting:

☐ Monday - Jeremiah 43 & Psalm 96

☐ Tuesday - Jeremiah 44 & Ecclesiastes 7:1-8:1

☐ Wednesday - Jeremiah 45 & Ecclesiastes 8:2-8

☐ Thursday - Jeremiah 46:1-12 & Ecclesiastes 8:9-9:12

☐ Friday - Jeremiah 46:13-28 & Ecclesiastes 9:13-10:20

☐ Saturday/Sunday - Ecclesiastes 11:1-12:14

Prayer Requests & Praise Reports

3-Year Bible Reading Plan
Year 2 Week 48

Week starting:

Monday - Jeremiah 47:1-48:10 & Psalm 97

Tuesday - Jeremiah 48:11-24 & Song of Songs 1:1-2:13

Wednesday - Jeremiah 48:25-47 & Song of Songs 2:14-3:5

Thursday - Jeremiah 49:1-6

Friday - Jeremiah 49:7-22

Saturday/Sunday - Jeremiah 49:23-39

Prayer Requests & Praise Reports

3-Year Bible Reading Plan
Year 2 Week 49

Week starting:

▢ Monday - Jeremiah 50:1-10 & Psalm 98

▢ Tuesday - Jeremiah 50:11-20 & Song of Songs 3:6-5:1

▢ Wednesday - Jeremiah 50:21-46 & Song of Songs 5:2-6:3

▢ Thursday - Jeremiah 51:1-14

▢ Friday - Jeremiah 51:15-19

▢ Saturday/Sunday - Jeremiah 51:20-23

Prayer Requests & Praise Reports

3-Year Bible Reading Plan
Year 2 Week 50

Week starting:

Monday - Jeremiah 51:24-35 & Psalm 99

Tuesday - Jeremiah 51:36-44 & Song of Songs 6:4-8:4

Wednesday - Jeremiah 51:45-53

Thursday - Jeremiah 51:54-52:11

Friday - Jeremiah 52:12-23

Saturday/Sunday - Jeremiah 52:24-34

Prayer Requests & Praise Reports

3-Year Bible Reading Plan
Year 2 Week 51

Week starting:

☐ Monday - Lamentations 1 & Psalm 100

☐ Tuesday - Lamentations 2 & Song of Songs 8:5-14

☐ Wednesday - Lamentations 3:1-24

☐ Thursday - Lamentations 3:25-66

☐ Friday - Lamentations 4

☐ Saturday/Sunday - Lamentations 5

Prayer Requests & Praise Reports

3-Year Bible Reading Plan
Year 2 Week 52

Week starting:

☐ Monday - *As the Lord leads*

☐ Tuesday - *As the Lord leads*

☐ Wednesday - *As the Lord leads*

☐ Thursday - *As the Lord leads*

☐ Friday - *As the Lord leads*

☐ Saturday/Sunday - *As the Lord leads*

Prayer Requests & Praise Reports

3-Year Bible Reading Plan
Year 3 Week 1

Week starting:

Monday - 1 Kings 1:1-4 & Psalm 101

Tuesday - 1 Kings 1:5-10 & Ezekiel 1

Wednesday - 1 Kings 5:11-53 & Ezekiel 2:1-3:15

Thursday - 1 Kings 2:1-12 & Ezekiel 3:16-4:17

Friday - 1 Kings 2:13-25 & Ezekiel 5

Saturday/Sunday - 1 Kings 2:26-35 & Ezekiel 6:1-7:13

Prayer Requests & Praise Reports

3-Year Bible Reading Plan
Year 3 Week 2

Week starting:

▢ Monday - 1 Kings 2:36-46 & Psalm 102

▢ Tuesday - 1 Kings 3:1-15 & Ezekiel 7:14-27

▢ Wednesday - 1 Kings 3:16-28 & Ezekiel 8:1-9:11

▢ Thursday - 1 Kings 4:1-19 & Ezekiel 10

▢ Friday - 1 Kings 4:20-34 & Ezekiel 11

▢ Saturday/Sunday - 1 Kings 5 & Ezekiel 12

Prayer Requests & Praise Reports

3-Year Bible Reading Plan
Year 3 Week 3

Week starting:

☐ Monday - 1 Kings 6:1-13 & Psalm 103

☐ Tuesday - 1 Kings 6:14-38 & Ezekiel 13:1-14:11

☐ Wednesday - 1 Kings 7:1-12 & Ezekiel 14:12-15:8

☐ Thursday - 1 Kings 7:13-26 & Ezekiel 16:1-34

☐ Friday - 1 Kings 7:27-51 & Ezekiel 16:35-52

☐ Saturday/Sunday - 1 Kings 8:1-13 & Ezekiel 16:53-17:10

Prayer Requests & Praise Reports

3-Year Bible Reading Plan
Year 3 Week 4

Week starting:

Monday - 1 Kings 8:14-21 & Psalm 104

Tuesday - 1 Kings 8:22-53 & Ezekiel 17:11-24

Wednesday - 1 Kings 8:54-66 & Ezekiel 18

Thursday - Ezekiel 19

Friday - 1 Kings 9:1-14 & Ezekiel 20:1-26

Saturday/Sunday - 1 Kings 9:15-28 & Ezekiel 20:27-49

Prayer Requests & Praise Reports

3-Year Bible Reading Plan
Year 3 Week 5

Week starting:

☐ Monday - 1 Kings 10:1-13 & Psalm 105

☐ Tuesday - 1 Kings 10:14-29 & Ezekiel 21:1-27

☐ Wednesday - 1 Kings 11:1-13 & Ezekiel 21:28-22:16

☐ Thursday - 1 Kings 11:14-25 & Ezekiel 22:17-23:21

☐ Friday - 1 Kings 11:26-43 & Ezekiel 23:22-35

☐ Saturday/Sunday - 1 Kings 12:1-20 & Ezekiel 23:36-24:14

Prayer Requests & Praise Reports

3-Year Bible Reading Plan
Year 3 Week 6

Week starting:

☐ Monday - 1 Kings 12:21-24 & Psalm 106

☐ Tuesday - 1 Kings 12:25-33 & Ezekiel 24:15-25:7

☐ Wednesday - 1 Kings 13 & Ezekiel 25:8-17

☐ Thursday - Ezekiel 26

☐ Friday - 1 Kings 14:1-20 & Ezekiel 27

☐ Saturday/Sunday - 1 Kings 14:21-31 & Ezekiel 28

Prayer Requests & Praise Reports

3-Year Bible Reading Plan
Year 3 Week 7

Week starting:

☐ Monday - 1 Kings 15:1-8 & Psalm 107

☐ Tuesday - 1 Kings 15:9-24 & Ezekiel 29

☐ Wednesday - 1 Kings 15:25-31 & Ezekiel 30

☐ Thursday - 1 Kings 15:32-16:20 & Ezekiel 31

☐ Friday - 1 Kings 16:21-28 & Ezekiel 32:1-16

☐ Saturday/Sunday - 1 Kings 16:29-17:7 & Ezekiel 32:17-33:9

Prayer Requests & Praise Reports

3-Year Bible Reading Plan
Year 3 Week 8

Week starting:

☐ Monday - 1 Kings 17:8-24 & Psalm 108

☐ Tuesday - 1 Kings 18:1-40 & Ezekiel 33:10-20

☐ Wednesday - 1 Kings 18:41-46 & Ezekiel 33:21-33

☐ Thursday - 1 Kings 19:1-18 & Ezekiel 34

☐ Friday - 1 Kings 19:19-21 & Ezekiel 35

☐ Saturday/Sunday - 1 Kings 20 :1-22 & Ezekiel 36:1-15

Prayer Requests & Praise Reports

3-Year Bible Reading Plan
Year 3 Week 9

Week starting:

☐ Monday - 1 Kings 20:23-34 & Psalm 109

☐ Tuesday - 1 Kings 20:35-43 & Ezekiel 36:16-38

☐ Wednesday - 1 Kings 21 & Ezekiel 37:1-14

☐ Thursday - 1 Kings 22:1-28 & Ezekiel 37:15-28

☐ Friday - 1 Kings 22:29-40 & Ezekiel 38

☐ Saturday/Sunday - 1 Kings 22:41-53 & Ezekiel 39:1-24

Prayer Requests & Praise Reports

3-Year Bible Reading Plan
Year 3 Week 10

Week starting:

☐ Monday - 2 Kings 1 & Psalm 110

☐ Tuesday - 2 Kings 2:1-18 & Ezekiel 39:25-29

☐ Wednesday - 2 Kings 2:19-25 & Ezekiel 40:1-4

☐ Thursday - 2 Kings 3 & Ezekiel 40:5-19

☐ Friday - 2 Kings 4:1-7 & Ezekiel 40:20-27

☐ Saturday/Sunday - 2 Kings 4:8-37 & Ezekiel 40:28-37

Prayer Requests & Praise Reports

3-Year Bible Reading Plan
Year 3 Week 11

Week starting:

☐ Monday - 2 Kings 4:38-44 & Psalm 111

☐ Tuesday - 2 Kings 5 & Ezekiel 40:38-49

☐ Wednesday - 2 Kings 6:1-7 & Ezekiel 41

☐ Thursday - 2 Kings 6:8-23 & Ezekiel 42

☐ Friday - 2 Kings 6:24-7:2 & Ezekiel 43:1-12

☐ Saturday/Sunday - 2 Kings 7:3-20 & Ezekiel 43:13-27

Prayer Requests & Praise Reports

3-Year Bible Reading Plan
Year 3 Week 12

Week starting:

▢ Monday - 2 Kings 8:1-6 & Psalm 112

▢ Tuesday - 2 Kings 8:7-15 7 Ezekiel 44:1-14

▢ Wednesday - 2 Kings 8:16-29 & Ezekiel 44:15-31

▢ Thursday - 2 Kings 9:1-13 & Ezekiel 45:1-8

▢ Friday - 2 Kings 9:14-29 & Ezekiel 45:9-25

▢ Saturday/Sunday - 2 Kings 9:30-37 & Ezekiel 46:1-18

Prayer Requests & Praise Reports

3-Year Bible Reading Plan
Year 3 Week 13

Week starting:

☐ Monday - 2 Kings 10:1-17 & Psalm 113

☐ Tuesday - 2 Kings 10:18-35 & Ezekiel 46:19-24

☐ Wednesday - 2 Kings 11:1-16 & Ezekiel 47:1-12

☐ Thursday - 2 Kings 11:17-21 & Ezekiel 47:13-23

☐ Friday - 2 Kings 12 & Ezekiel 48:1-22

☐ Saturday/Sunday - 2 Kings 13:1-9 & Ezekiel 48:23-25

Prayer Requests & Praise Reports

3-Year Bible Reading Plan
Year 3 Week 14

Week starting:

Monday - 2 Kings 13:10-13 & Psalm 114

Tuesday - 2 Kings 13:14-25 & Daniel 1

Wednesday - 2 Kings 14:1-22 & Daniel 2:1-23

Thursday - 2 Kings 14:23-29 & Daniel 2:24-45

Friday - Daniel 2:46-3:18

Saturday/Sunday - 2 Kings 15:1-12 & Daniel 3:19-4:18

Prayer Requests & Praise Reports

3-Year Bible Reading Plan
Year 3 Week 15

Week starting:

☐ Monday - 2 Kings 15 :13-22 & Psalm 115

☐ Tuesday - 2 Kings 15:23-31 & Daniel 4:19-33

☐ Wednesday - 2 Kings 15:32-38 & Daniel 4:34-5:31

☐ Thursday - Daniel 6

☐ Friday - 2 Kinsg 16 & Daniel 7:1-14

☐ Saturday/Sunday - 2 Kings 17:1-4 & Daniel 7:15-8:14

Prayer Requests & Praise Reports

3-Year Bible Reading Plan
Year 3 Week 16

Week starting:

☐ Monday - 2 Kings 17:5-23 & Psalm 116

☐ Tuesday - 2 Kings 17:24-41 & Daniel 8:15-9:19

☐ Wednesday - 2 Kings 18:1-12 & Daniel 9:20-27

☐ Thursday - 2 Kings 18:13-37 & Daniel 10:1-11:1

☐ Friday - 2 Kings 19:1-19 & Daniel 11:2-20

☐ Saturday/Sunday - 2 Kings 19:20-37 & Daniel 11:21-12:13

Prayer Requests & Praise Reports

3-Year Bible Reading Plan
Year 3 Week 17

Week starting:

☐ Monday - 2 Kings 20:1-11 & Psalm 117

☐ Tuesday - 2 Kings 20:12-21 & John 1:1-18

☐ Wednesday - John 1:19-50

☐ Thursday - 2 Kings 21:1-18 & John 2:1-12

☐ Friday - 2 Kings 21:19-22:7 & John 2:13-25

☐ Saturday/Sunday - 2 Kings 22:8-20 & John 3:1-36

Prayer Requests & Praise Reports

3-Year Bible Reading Plan
Year 3 Week 18

Week starting:

Monday - 2 Kings 23:1-20 & Psalm 118

Tuesday - 2 Kings 23:21-33 & John 3:31-36

Wednesday - 2 Kings 23:34-24:7 & John 4:1-42

Thursday - John 4:43-5:15

Friday - John 5:16-30

Saturday/Sunday - John 5:31-47

Prayer Requests & Praise Reports

3-Year Bible Reading Plan
Year 3 Week 19

Week starting:

☐ Monday - Psalm 119:1-88

☐ Tuesday - 2 Kings 24:8-17 & John 6:1-21

☐ Wednesday - 2 Kings 24:18-25:7 & John 6:22-59

☐ Thursday - 2 Kings 25:8-21 & John 6:60-7:9

☐ Friday - 2 Kings 25:22-26 & John 7:10-35

☐ Saturday/Sunday - 2 Kings 25:27-30 & John 7:36-53

Prayer Requests & Praise Reports

3-Year Bible Reading Plan
Year 3 Week 20

Week starting:

☐ Monday - 1 Chronicles 1:1-27 & Psalm 119:89-176

☐ Tuesday - 1 Chronicles 1:28-33 & John 8:1-11

☐ Wednesday - 1 Chronicles 1:34-42 & John 8:12-30

☐ Thursday - 1 Chronicles 1:43-54 & John 8:13-59

☐ Friday - 1 Chronicles 2:1-8 & John 9:1-34

☐ Saturday/Sunday - 1 Chronicles 2:9-17 & John 9:35-41

Prayer Requests & Praise Reports

3-Year Bible Reading Plan
Year 3 Week 21

Week starting:

Monday - 1 Chronicles 2:18-24 & Psalm 120

Tuesday - 1 Chronicles 2:25-41 & John 10:1-21

Wednesday - 1 Chronicles 2:42-55 & John 10:22-42

Thursday - 1 Chronicles 3:1-9 & John 11:1-44

Friday - 1 Chronicles 3:10-24 & John 11:45-57

Saturday/Sunday - 1 Chronicles 4:1-20

Prayer Requests & Praise Reports

3-Year Bible Reading Plan
Year 3 Week 22

Week starting:

☐ Monday - Psalm 121

☐ Tuesday - 1 Chronicles 4:21-23 & John 12:1-19

☐ Wednesday - 1 Chronicles 4:24-43 & John 12:20-50

☐ Thursday - 1 Chronicles 5:1-10 & John 13:1-17

☐ Friday - 1 Chronicles 5:11-17 & John 13:18-38

☐ Saturday/Sunday - 1 Chronicles 5:18-26 & John 14:1-14

Prayer Requests & Praise Reports

3-Year Bible Reading Plan
Year 3 Week 23

Week starting:

☐ Monday - Psalm 122

☐ Tuesday - 1 Chronicles 6:1-15 & John 14:15-31

☐ Wednesday - 1 Chronicles 6:16-30 & John 15:1-17

☐ Thursday - 1 Chronicles 6:31-48 & John 15:18-16:4

☐ Friday - 1 Chronicles 6:49-53 & John 16:5-15

☐ Saturday/Sunday - 1 Chronicles 6:54-81 & John 16:16-33

Prayer Requests & Praise Reports

3-Year Bible Reading Plan
Year 3 Week 24

Week starting:

Monday - 1 Chronicles 7:1-5 & Psalm 123

Tuesday - 1 Chronicles 7:6-12 & John 17

Wednesday - 1 Chronicles 7:13-19 & John 18:1-14

Thursday - 1 Chronicles 7:20-29 & John 18:15-27

Friday - 1 Chronicles 7:30-40 & John 18:28-40

Saturday/Sunday - 1 Chronicles 8:1-28 & John 19:1-16

Prayer Requests & Praise Reports

3-Year Bible Reading Plan
Year 3 Week 25

Week starting:

☐ Monday - 1 Chronicles 8:29-40 & Psalm 124

☐ Tuesday - John 19:17-37

☐ Wednesday - 1 Chronicles 9:1-9 & John 19:38-20:10

☐ Thursday - 1 Chronicles 9:10-13 & John 20:11-29

☐ Friday - 1 Chronicles 9:14-34 & John 20:30-21:14

☐ Saturday/Sunday - 1 Chronicles 9:35-44 & John 21:15-25

Prayer Requests & Praise Reports

3-Year Bible Reading Plan
Year 3 Week 26

Week starting:

☐ Monday - 1 Chronicles 10 & Psalm 125

☐ Tuesday - 1 Chronicles 10 & Hosea 1

☐ Wednesday - 1 Chronicles 11:1-9 & Hosea 2:1-13

☐ Thursday - 1 Chronicles 11:10-47 & Hosea 2:14-3:5

☐ Friday - 1 Chronicles 12:1-7 & Hosea 4:1-10

☐ Saturday/Sunday - 1 Chronicles 12:8-15 & Hosea 4:11-19

Prayer Requests & Praise Reports

3-Year Bible Reading Plan
Year 3 Week 27

Week starting:

◻ Monday - 1 Chronicles 12:16-18 & Psalm 126

_____

_____

_____

◻ Tuesday - 1 Chronicles 12:19-22 & Hosea 5

_____

_____

_____

◻ Wednesday - 1 Chronicles 12:23-40 & Hosea 6

_____

_____

_____

◻ Thursday - 1 Chronicles 13 & Hosea 7

_____

_____

_____

◻ Friday - 1 Chornicles 14:1-7 & Hosea 8

_____

_____

_____

◻ Saturday/Sunday - 1 Chornicles 14:8-17 & Hosea 9

_____

_____

_____

Prayer Requests & Praise Reports

_____

_____

_____

3-Year Bible Reading Plan
Year 3 Week 28

Week starting:

▢ Monday - 1 Chronicles 15:1-24 & Psalm 127

▢ Tuesday - 1 Chronicles 15:25-16:6 & Hosea 10

▢ Wednesday - 1 Chronicles 16:7-36 & Hosea 11:1-11

▢ Thursday - 1 Chornicles 16:37-43 & Hosea 11:12-12:14

▢ Friday - 1 Chronicles 17:1-15 & Hosea 13

▢ Saturday/Sunday - 1 Chronicles 17:16-27 & Hosea 14

Prayer Requests & Praise Reports

3-Year Bible Reading Plan
Year 3 Week 29

Week starting:

☐ Monday - 1 Chronicles 18 & Psalm 128

☐ Tuesday - 1 Chronicles 19 & Joel 1

☐ Wednesday - 1 Chronicles 20:1-3 & Joel 2:1-11

☐ Thursday - 1 Chronicles 20:4-8 & Joel 2:12-17

☐ Friday - 1 Chronicles 21:1-22:1 & Joel 2:18-32

☐ Saturday/Sunday - 1 Chronicles 22:2-19 & Joel 3:1-16

Prayer Requests & Praise Reports

3-Year Bible Reading Plan
Year 3 Week 30

Week starting:

☐ Monday - 1 Chronicles 23 & Psalm 129

☐ Tuesday - 1 Chronicles 24:1-19 & Joel 3:17-21

☐ Wednesday - 1 Chronicles 24:20-31 & Amos 1:1-2:3

☐ Thursday - 1 Chronicles 25 & Amos 2:4-3:15

☐ Friday - 1 Chronicles 26:1-19 & Amos 4

☐ Saturday/Sunday - 1 Chronicles 26:20-32 & Amos 5:1-17

Prayer Requests & Praise Reports

3-Year Bible Reading Plan
Year 3 Week 31

Week starting:

Monday - 1 Chronicles 27:1-15 & Psalm 130

Tuesday - 1 Chronicles 27:16-24 & Amos 5:18-6:14

Wednesday - 1 Chronicles 27:25-34 & Amos 7:1-6

Thursday - 1 Chronicles 28 & Amos 7:7-17

Friday - 1 Chronicles 29:1-9 & Amos 8

Saturday/Sunday - 1 Chronicles 29:10-30 & Amos 9

Prayer Requests & Praise Reports

3-Year Bible Reading Plan
Year 3 Week 32

Week starting:

☐ Monday - 2 Chronicles 1 & Psalm 131

☐ Tuesday - 2 Chronicles 2 & Obadiah 1:1-9

☐ Wednesday - 2 Chronicles 3 & Obadiah 1:10-21

☐ Thursday - 2 Chronicles 4:1-5:1 & Jonah 1

☐ Friday - 2 Chronicles 5:2-14 & Jonah 2

☐ Saturday/Sunday - 2 Chronicles 6:1-11 & Jonah 3:1-4:11

Prayer Requests & Praise Reports

3-Year Bible Reading Plan
Year 3 Week 33

Week starting:

☐ Monday - Psalm 132

☐ Tuesday - 2 Chronicles 6:12-42 & Micah 1

☐ Wednesday - 2 Chronicles 7:1-10 & Micah 2

☐ Thursday - 2 Chronicles 7:11-22 & Micah 3

☐ Friday - 2 Chronicles 8 & Micah 4:1-5

☐ Saturday/Sunday - 2 Chronicles 9:1-12

Prayer Requests & Praise Reports

3-Year Bible Reading Plan
Year 3 Week 34

Week starting:

Monday - 2 Chronicles 9:13-31 & Psalm 133

Tuesday - Micah 4:6-5:1

Wednesday - 2 Chronicles 10 & Micah 5:2-15

Thursday - 2 Chronicles 11 & Micah 6

Friday - Micah 7

Saturday/Sunday - 2 Chronicles 12

Prayer Requests & Praise Reports

3-Year Bible Reading Plan
Year 3 Week 35

Week starting:

☐ Monday - 2 Chronicles 13 & Psalm 134

☐ Tuesday - 2 Chronicles 14 & Hebrews 1:1-2:18

☐ Wednesday - 2 Chronicles 15 & Hebrews 3:1-4:13

☐ Thursday - 2 Chronicles 16 & Hebrews 4:14-5:10

☐ Friday - 2 Chronicles 17 & Hebrews 5:11-7:14

☐ Saturday/Sunday - Hebrews 7:15-8:13

Prayer Requests & Praise Reports

3-Year Bible Reading Plan
Year 3 Week 36

Week starting:

Monday - 2 Chronicles 18:1-27 & Psalm 135

Tuesday - 2 Chronicles 18:28-19:11 & Hebrews 9

Wednesday - Hebrews 10

Thursday - 2 Chronicles 20:1-30 & Hebrews 11

Friday - 2 Chronicles 20:31-37 & Hebrews 12

Saturday/Sunday - 2 Chronicles 21 & Hebrews 13

Prayer Requests & Praise Reports

3-Year Bible Reading Plan
Year 3 Week 37

Week starting:

- Monday - 2 Chronicles 22:1-9 & Psalm 136

- Tuesday - 2 Chronicles 22:10-12 & James 1:1-18

- Wednesday - 2 Chronicles 23:1-15 & James 1:19-27

- Thursday - 2 Chronicles 23:16-21 & James 2:1-13

- Friday - 2 Chronicles 24:1-16 & James 2:14-26

- Saturday/Sunday - 2 Chronicles 24:17-22 & James 3:1-12

Prayer Requests & Praise Reports

3-Year Bible Reading Plan
Year 3 Week 38

Week starting:

☐ Monday - 2 Chronicles 24:23-27 & Psalm 137

☐ Tuesday - 2 Chronicles 25 & James 3:13-18

☐ Wednesday - James 4:1-10

☐ Thursday - 2 Chronicles 26:1-15 & James 4:11-17

☐ Friday - 2 Chronicles 26:16-23 & James 5:1-6

☐ Saturday/Sunday - 2 Chronicles 27 & James 5:7-20

Prayer Requests & Praise Reports

3-Year Bible Reading Plan
Year 3 Week 39

Week starting:

Monday - 2 Chronicles 28:1-15 & Psalm 138

Tuesday - 2 Chronicles 28:16-27 & 1 Peter 1:1-12

Wednesday - 2 Chronicles 29:1-17 & 1 Peter 1:13-2:12

Thursday - 2 Chronicles 29:18-36 & 1 Peter 2:13-25

Friday - 2 Chronicles 30:1-9 & 1 Peter 3

Saturday/Sunday - 2 Chronicles 30:10-27 & 1 Peter 4:1-11

Prayer Requests & Praise Reports

3-Year Bible Reading Plan
Year 3 Week 40

Week starting:

☐ Monday - Psalm 139

☐ Tuesday - 2 Chronicles 31 & 1 Peter 4:12-5:14

☐ Wednesday - 2 Chronicles 32:1-23 & 2 Peter 1:1-11

☐ Thursday - 2 Chronicles 32:24-33 & 2 Peter 1:12-21

☐ Friday - 2 Peter 2

☐ Saturday/Sunday - 2 Peter 3

Prayer Requests & Praise Reports

3-Year Bible Reading Plan
Year 3 Week 41

Week starting:

☐ Monday - 2 Chronicles 33:1-20 & Psalm 140

☐ Tuesday - 2 Chronicles 33:21-15 & 1 John 1:1-2:6

☐ Wednesday - 1 John 2:7-17

☐ Thursday - 2 Chronicles 34:1-13 & 1 John 2:18-3:10

☐ Friday - 2 Chronicles 34:14-28 & & 1 John 3:11-24

☐ Saturday/Sunday - 2 Chronicles 34:29-33 & 1 John4

Prayer Requests & Praise Reports

3-Year Bible Reading Plan
Year 3 Week 42

Week starting:

◻ Monday - 2 Chronicles 35:1-19 & Psalm 141

◻ Tuesday - 2 Chronicles 35:20-27 & 1 John 5

◻ Wednesday - 2 Chronicles 36:1-10 & 2 John

◻ Thursday - 2 Chronicles 36:11-23 & 3 John

◻ Friday - Jude 1-16

◻ Saturday/Sunday - Jude 17-25

Prayer Requests & Praise Reports

3-Year Bible Reading Plan
Year 3 Week 43

Week starting:

Monday - Ezra 1 & Psalm 142

Tuesday - Ezra 2 & Nahum 1

Wednesday - Ezra 3:1-6 & Nahum 2:1-3:19

Thursday - Ezra 3:7-13 & Habakkuk 1

Friday - Ezra 4:1-5 & Habakkuk 2

Saturday/Sunday - Ezra 4:6-23 & Habakkuk 3

Prayer Requests & Praise Reports

3-Year Bible Reading Plan
Year 3 Week 44

Week starting:

☐ Monday - Ezra 4:24-5:17 & Psalm 143

☐ Tuesday - Ezra 6:1-5 & Zephaniah 1

☐ Wednesday - Ezra 6:6-18 & Zephaniah 2

☐ Thursday - Ezra 6:19-7:10 & Zephaniah 3

☐ Friday - Ezra 7:11-26 & Haggai 1

☐ Saturday/Sunday - Ezra 7:27-8:14 & Haggai 2

Prayer Requests & Praise Reports

3-Year Bible Reading Plan
Year 3 Week 45

Week starting:

☐ Monday - Ezra 8:15-36 & Psalm 144

☐ Tuesday - Zechariah 1

☐ Wednesday - Zechariah 2:1-3:10

☐ Thursday - Ezra 9 & Zechariah 4

☐ Friday - Ezra 10:1-17 & Zechariah 5:1-6:15

☐ Saturday/Sunday - Ezra 10:18-44 & Zechariah 7

Prayer Requests & Praise Reports

3-Year Bible Reading Plan
Year 3 Week 46

Week starting:

☐ Monday - Nehemiah 1 & Psalm 145

☐ Tuesday - Nehemiah 2 & Zechariah 8:1-9:8

☐ Wednesday - Nehemiah 3 & Zechariah 9:9-17

☐ Thursday - Zechariah 10:1-11:3

☐ Friday - Zechariah 11:4-17

☐ Saturday/Sunday - Nehemiah 4 & Zechariah 12:1-13:9

Prayer Requests & Praise Reports

3-Year Bible Reading Plan
Year 3 Week 47

Week starting:

☐ Monday - Psalm 146

☐ Tuesday - Nehemiah 5 & Zechariah 14

☐ Wednesday - Nehemiah 6:1-14 & Malachi 1:1-5

☐ Thursday - Nehemiah 6:15-7:3 & Malachi 1:6-2:9

☐ Friday - Nehemiah 7:4-73 & Malachi 2:10-3:5

☐ Saturday/Sunday - Nehemiah 8:1-12 & Malachi 3:6-4:6

Prayer Requests & Praise Reports

3-Year Bible Reading Plan
Year 3 Week 48

Week starting:

☐ Monday - Nehemiah 8:13-18 & Psalm 147

☐ Tuesday - Nehemiah 9:1-37

☐ Wednesday - Revelation 1

☐ Thursday - Revelation 2:1-17

☐ Friday - Nehemiah 9:38-10:27 & Revelation 2:18-3:6

☐ Saturday/Sunday - Nehemiah 10:28-39 & Revelation 3:7-22

Prayer Requests & Praise Reports

3-Year Bible Reading Plan
Year 3 Week 49

Week starting:

Monday - Nehemiah 11 & Psalm 148

Tuesday - Nehemiah 12:1-26 & Revelation 4:1-5:14

Wednesday - Revelation 6:1-7:17

Thursday - Nehemiah 12:27-43 & Revelation 8:1-9:21

Friday - Nehemiah 12:44-48 & Revelation 10

Saturday/Sunday - Nehemiah 13 & Revelation 11

Prayer Requests & Praise Reports

3-Year Bible Reading Plan
Year 3 Week 50

Week starting:

☐ Monday - Esther 1 & Psalm 149

☐ Tuesday - Esther 2 & Revelation 12

☐ Wednesday - Revelation 13:1-14:13

☐ Thursday - Esther 3 & Revelation 14:14-15:8

☐ Friday - Esther 4 & Revelation 16

☐ Saturday/Sunday - Esther 5:1-8 & Revelation 17

Prayer Requests & Praise Reports

3-Year Bible Reading Plan
Year 3 Week 51

Week starting:

☐ Monday - Esther 5:9-14 & Psalm 150

☐ Tuesday - Esther 6 & Revelation 18

☐ Wednesday - Esther 7 & Revelation 19

☐ Thursday - Esther 8 & Revelation 20

☐ Friday - Esther 9:1-19 & Revelation 21:1-22:6

☐ Saturday/Sunday - Esther 9:20-10:3 & Revelation 22:7-21

Prayer Requests & Praise Reports

3-Year Bible Reading Plan
Year 3 Week 52

Week starting:

☐ Monday - *As the Lord leads*

☐ Tuesday - *As the Lord leads*

☐ Wednesday - *As the Lord leads*

☐ Thursday - *As the Lord leads*

☐ Friday - *As the Lord leads*

☐ Saturday/Sunday - *As the Lord leads*

Prayer Requests & Praise Reports

Made in the USA
Monee, IL
20 May 2025

17830244R00090